Pebble Plus

Animal Offspring

Dogs and Their Puppies

Revised Edition

T0044782

by Linda Tagliaferro

CAPSTONE PRESS
a capstone imprint

Pebble Plus is published by Capstone Press,
1710 Roe Crest Drive,
North Mankato, Minnesota 56003
www.capstonepub.com

Copyright © 2018 by Capstone Press, a Capstone imprint. All rights reserved. No part of this publication may be reproduced in whole or in part, or stored in a retrieval system, or transmitted in any form or by any means, electronic, mechanical, photocopying, recording, or otherwise, without written permission of the publisher.

Library of Congress Cataloging-in-Publication Data
Names: Tagliaferro, Linda, author. Title: Dogs and their puppies : a 4D book / by Linda Tagliaferro. Description: Revised edition. | North Mankato, Minnesota : Capstone Press, a Capstone imprint, [2018] | Series: Pebble plus. animal offspring | Includes bibliographical references and index.
Identifiers: LCCN 2017037870 (print) | LCCN 2017052293 (ebook) | ISBN 9781543508628 (eBook PDF) | ISBN 9781543508222 (hardcover) | ISBN 9781543508345 (pbk.)
Subjects: LCSH: Puppies—Juvenile literature. | Dogs—Juvenile literature.
Classification: LCC SF426.5 (ebook) | LCC SF426.5 .T34 2018 (print) | DDC 636.7/07—dc23 LC record available at https://lccn.loc.gov/2017037870

Editorial Credits
Gina Kammer, editor; Sarah Bennett, designer;
Morgan Walters, media researcher;
Katy LaVigne, production specialist

Photo Credits
Shutterstock: Anna Goroshnikova, right 21, Anna Hoychuk, 15, Burry van den Brink, 19 , Christian Mueller, Cover, Fernando Castelani, right 20, left 21, framsook, 5, Grigorita Ko, 3, 17, Kristin Castenschiold, 7, Nadya Chetah, 9, Nixx Photography, left 20, Sarune Kairyte, 11, Stephen Coburn, 13

Note to Parents and Teachers

The Animal Offspring set supports national science standards related to life sciences. This book describes and illustrates dogs and their puppies. The images support early readers in understanding the text.
The repetition of words and phrases helps early readers learn new words. This book also introduces early readers to subject-specific vocabulary words, which are defined in the Glossary section. Early readers may need assistance to read some words and to use the Table of Contents, Glossary, Read More, Internet Sites, Critical Thinking Questions, and Index sections of the book.

Printed in the United States 5612

Table of Contents

Dogs 4

Puppies 8

Growing Up 14

Watch Dogs Grow. 20

Glossary 22

Read More. 23

Internet Sites 23

Critical Thinking Questions 24

Index 24

Dogs

Dogs are mammals.

Young dogs are

called puppies.

Male and female dogs mate.

Female dogs give birth

to a litter of puppies.

Puppies

Puppies cannot see
or hear until they are
about ten days old.

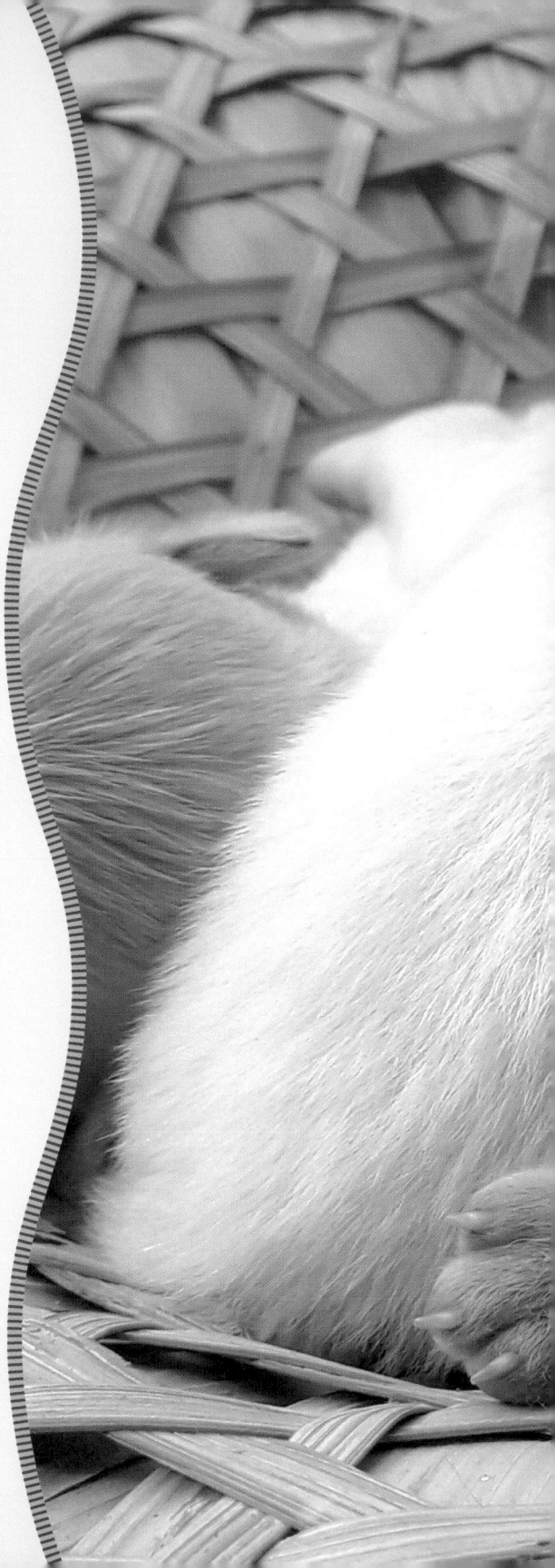

Puppies sleep most of the time. Puppies get tired from playing.

Puppies drink milk
from their mother
for about five weeks.

Growing Up

Puppies can eat dog food when they are about six weeks old.

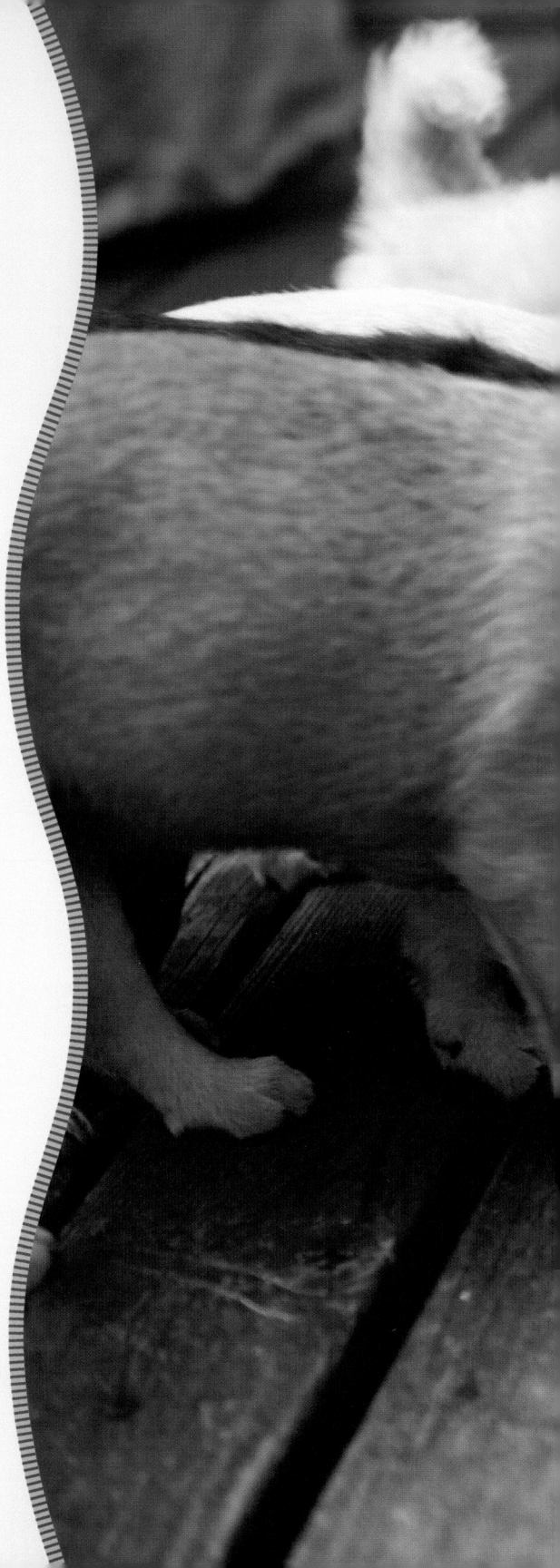

Puppies jump on and
play with each other.
They chew toys.

Puppies become adults
after one to two years.

Watch Dogs Grow

birth

adult after
about two years

Glossary

adult—an animal that is able to mate

litter—a group of puppies born at the same time to the same mother; dogs usually have litters of four to six puppies

mammal—a warm-blooded animal that has a backbone; most mammals have hair or fur; female mammals feed milk to their young

mate—to join together to produce young

Read More

Carr, Aaron. *Dogs.* Science Kids: Life Cycles. New York: AV2 by Weigl, 2016.

Lynch, Annabelle. *Dogs and Puppies.* Animals and Their Babies. Mankato, Minn.: A+ Smart Apple Media, 2017.

Swinney, Nicola Jane. *My Little Book of Dogs and Puppies.* New York: Sandy Creek, 2016.

Internet Sites

Use FactHound to find Internet sites related to this book.

Visit *www.facthound.com*

Just type **9781543508222** and go.

Critical Thinking Questions

1. What are puppies like right after they are born?
2. What is the word used for a group of puppies born at the same time?
3. How do puppies change as they grow into dogs?

Index

adults, 18
birth, 6
chewing, 16
eating, 14
females, 6
food, 14
hearing, 8
jumping, 16
litters, 6
males, 6
mammals, 4
mating, 6
milk, 12
mothers, 12
playing, 10, 16
seeing, 8
sleeping, 10
toys, 16